Stefan Luckhaus

Book Series
Increasing Productivity of Software Development

Part 2
Management Model, Cost Estimation and KPI Improvement

Internet: www.pass-consulting.com

Editing & Proofreading:
Heidrun Fernau-Rienecker, Anelka Dudaczy

Cover Design & Typesetting:
Antje Schwarzbauer

Cover Graphic & Photos:
Shutterstock Images LLC

Production & Distribution:
PASS IT-Consulting Dipl. Inf. G. Rienecker GmbH & Co. KG
Heidrun Fernau-Rienecker

Print:
tredition

Printed in Germany
June 2018

ISBN:
Hardcover: 978-3-9819565-2-8
Paperback: 978-3-9819565-5-9
e-Book: 978-3-9819565-3-5

Contents

Contents

Figures

Tables

Introduction:
Factories – from Manufactures
to Software Production

For software developing companies an increase of their productivity has the following effects [Wallmüller 1990]:

- Developing software products in shorter periods of time;
- Developing software products in order to achieve a higher return on invest;
- Developing software products with higher quality.

There is no doubt that these are desirable, in some cases even essential goals. For start-ups in their first rounds of financing, for example, exactly these aspects are crucial for the development of a digital business model and its rating by investors. The first question this book wants to answer is: To what extent can productivity be increased? In other words: Which improvements regarding these effects can be expected in practice?

The potential of productivity improvements

Today, a wide range of productivity values can be measured in the practice of software development. This is due to the fact that, compared to ohter industrial areas this sector is still lagging behind. Figure 1 shows measurements of PASS Consulting Group for different development paradigms, which have been calculated on the basis of the relationship of output to input. The output has been measured with the Data Interaction Point method (unit: DIP), the input in man-days (unit: MD) [Luckhaus 2014].

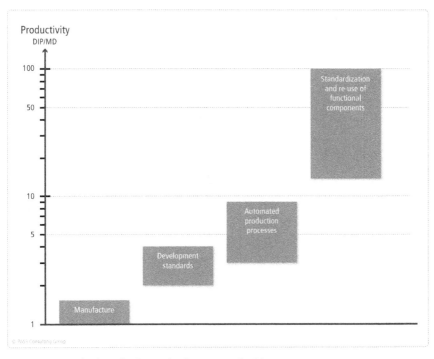

Figure 1: Empirical values of software development productivity

The manufacture – software as a handcraft

In the context of software development the term manufacture stands for a software producer with the following characteristics: software is created from scratch as a unique product, where the development process as well as the implemented functionality is unique and individual. The development process makes use of existing programming languages, compilers, environments, tools, and so on, but otherwise it is characterized by manual work – craftsmanship. Product and process quality highly depend on the experience and the skills of the developers.

PASS has experience with and productivity measurements from their own as well as from customer projects, where software has been developed in a manufacture-like manner. Usually, their productivity is just a little over 1 DIP/MD. Projects performing poorly can even have a productivity of less than 1 DIP/MD, while the best in class can reach a value of 2. A higher productivity cannot be expected of this type of software development.

Development standards

Productivity in software development increases if technical and process standards are defined and applied, for example:

- Programming guidelines and design patterns, supported by development environments which are integrated with version control systems, code analysis tools, and so on.
- Development frameworks with reusable technical components.
- Standard architectures which provide proven system components and facilitate the integration of the developed software with these system components as well as a subsequent exchange.

- Modern development paradigms which save implementation effort for new code by delegating tasks to the underlying platform and combine the strengths of, for example, object oriented and functional programming concepts.
- Process models determining processes and methods for all competence areas of software development, including templates for all documents that need to be created.

One advantage of standards is that some requirements can be fulfilled without having to implement or test individual code. Additionally, standards protect the investment in the software product because process and product meet predefined quality criteria and are independent of the experience and the skills of individual process participants. In case of industry standards, frameworks such as Hibernate, Spring, PrimeFaces, and so on, the developing company can benefit from industry-wide experience, making it far easier to recruit additional, qualified specialists for maintenance and further development tasks.

Productivity measurements of projects applying technical and process standards without automating sub-processes of software development, which have been performed by PASS Consulting Group, show values between 2 and 4 DIP/MD. Thus, compared to a project which, due to its handcrafted way of working, has a productivity of 1 DIP/MD, development standards can increase productivity by a factor of four. One advantage of this could be to generate the same output at a quarter of the costs, another to multiply functionality by four at the same costs.

Development standards are a first step from a manufacture to a factory and an important basis for the next milestone: increasing automation within the production process.

Automated production processes

Model-based development with automated code generation allows the implementation of software on the abstract level of a model instead of using a programming language. An example for this is the PASS Software Factory, where this paradigm is applied in commercial software development for about 20 years, under continual optimization based on productivity and quality measurements. It is based on models for dialogs, processes, workflows, data structures, interfaces and tools for the creation and modification of objects in these areas, for example ‚graphical user interfaces, data models, models of business objects, simple process flows, workflows with multiple user interactions, and so on. The developer can link the different models such as workflows with dialogs, buttons in dialogs with processes, input fields with data elements, and so on. Based on models and templates specifying language, style and commentation, a code generator creates executable code which is automatically enriched, for example, by technical validation checks. Later changes are performed on model level, while related code is generated automatically.

An empirical value derived from the development of individual software solutions with the PASS Software Factory states that about 80% of the code is generated code based on the models whereas about 20% need to be programmed individually. Productivity measured in different projects lies between 3 and 8 DIP/MD.

There is even more potential in standardization. Examples are a unified dialog layout where search dialogs with a result list and subsequent detail views are automatically generated from business objects or generated workflows with unified 4-eye or 6-eye approval procedures for selected business objects. This type of standardization does not exclude the consideration of individual requirements, but it simplifies their implementation. With standardized, model-driven and generative development, productivity values between 20 and 25 DIP/MD are possible.

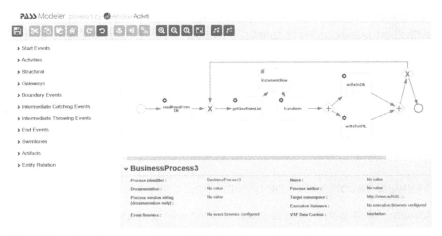

Figure 2: Modeling of a process with the PASS Software Factory (example)

The implementation of code is not the only area for automation approaches. Automation is possible throughout the whole development process. In projects working with the PASS Software Factory, business analysis and the creation of concepts are labeled as the most time-consuming areas. PASS is currently working on an enhancement of its modelling tools enabling business analysts to specify a planned system together with the customer, directly in the models of the Software Factory without the usual paperwork. Because these models are the source for code generation, this approach prevents errors caused by the interpretation of incomplete or ambiguous specifications.

After implementation, build and deploy processes can be automated easily. When considering a higher effort, this is even true for tests. With more standardization and code generation, the percentage of constructive quality assurance increases and the need for analytical quality assurance of individually implemented requirements decreases. Besides, the quality of manual tests strongly depends of the tester's thoroughness and is a cost driver if high test coverage must keep pace with short release cycles or sprints. To improve the area of testing PASS follows with its test factory, the approach of automated end-to-end tests, where test cases and related scripts are defined by a tester and executed automatically on demand or cyclic, for example, linked to a nightly build. Merely 2 to 3 test runs later, the effort for creating test cases and scripts has paid off. However, there is considerable potential for productivity improvement in the area of creating test cases and test data.

Standardization and reuse of functional components

Modern industrialized mass production is not only characterized by automation but also by standardization. At first, only the product itself was standardized, later increasingly smaller components, from which the product is built within the production process.

The automotive industry serves as a good example: The customers can configure a vehicle individually by selecting available options in almost any combination. Within the automated production, the selected components for each vehicle are put together according to the individual customer's choice. A vehicle leaving the production line rarely looks like another.

Additionally, effort in software development can be reduced if new systems are created by simply putting existing components with a clearly defined functionality together, making an individual coding of this functionality unnecessary. The smaller these components are, the more individual the created system. This paradigm requires every business or technical component to be available for others including a description of its functionality and the interface. Ideally, new requirements can simply be fulfilled by already existing components and personnel costs occur only for requirements analysis, orchestration and configuration of a system, which is significantly less than coding the functionality completely from scratch. Therefore, productivity as well as time to market, return on investment and quality achieve optimal values.

PASS Consulting Group has empirical values for this paradigm of software development, too. Shortly before this book was published a comprehensive travel management system was developed for a customer, with a size of 30,442 Data Interaction Points. Not only technical components have been reused for this system but also some from the so-called "Solution World Travel", an industry related functional component repository of PASS. In total, the degree of reusability was measured at 90% and the productivity at 80.7 DIP/MD (see also chapter "II. Application of measuring methods", "Measuring delivery- and new-development productivity"). If other paradigms were used instead of reusability, the development effort would be significantly higher:

Paradigm	Productivity	Effort
90% reusability (measured)	80.7 DIP/MD	377 MD
Model-based development (assumed)	8 DIP/MD	3,805 MD
Manufacture (assumed)	1 DIP/MD	30,442 MD

Table 1: Model calculation for development effort using different paradigms

Compared to a manufacture-like development, this type of development could save more than 30,000 man-days.

Considering this and similar development projects, the potential of reusability has not yet been fully exploited. More likely, it is a cautious first step, enabling improvements in two different directions:

- The horizontal extension of the component range towards a greater functional diversity.

- The granularity, which means the size of the standardized interchangeable components, in order to enable more individual combinations.

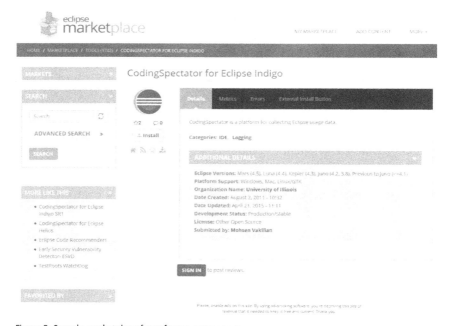

Figure 3: Sample marketplace for software components

In consequence, these improvements result in a wider pool of software components and in the challenge of bringing suppliers and demanders together. This calls for a central representation of all available components, including descriptions of their functionality and interfaces, adequate search features, and so on. With regard to open source components, plug-ins for large application systems, apps, and so on this challenge has already been solved by internet marketplaces (see figure 3) [Fettke/Loos/Viehweger 2003]. Currently, many companies, including PASS, develop own marketplaces in order to offer business and technical components coming from their different organizational units – initially for internal use, later often as a virtual sales channel.

A management model for optimizing productivity

The analysis of development projects which have been performed according to different paradigms not only shows the potential regarding productivity increases. It additionally makes clear that single improvement measures are not sufficient to improve productivity sustainably to this extent. For example, the introduction of a single modelling tool is no guarantee for the advantages a model-based development has to offer. All developers must be able to use it without difficulty. If modelling requires business and technical knowledge, different roles and skills are required, and the models must present a benefit for subsequent process steps – preferably without media breaks. However, it is possible that alleged improvement measures lead to a decreasing productivity. Chances are this doesn't become transparent until a new development is completed and further development begins.

Figure 4 shows a management model, which has been in use by PASS for many years. It allows objective control by targeting the exertion of influence and simultaneously controlling the own productivity. Its basis are measuring methods and a manageable number of key performance indicators (KPIs). Without these, a company can neither determine its own productivity nor detect if changes resulted in an improvement or a deterioration. To begin with, the following chapter describes the introduction and calibration of such measuring methods and KPIs. Subsequent chapters illustrate their cyclic application, evaluation and optimization in different key performance areas or rather by recalibrations of the measuring methods.

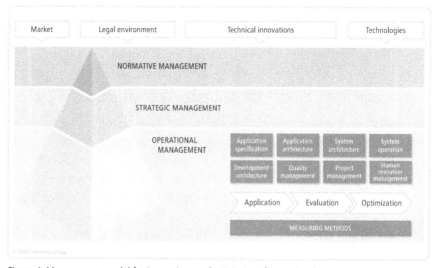

Figure 4: Management model for increasing productivity in software development

I. KPIs and Measuring Methods

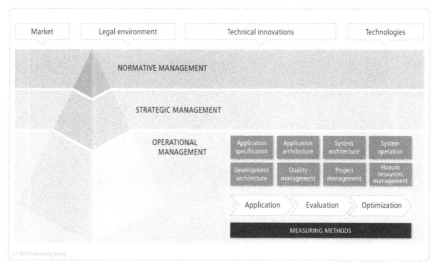

Figure 5: Measuring methods are the basis of the management model

The introduction begins with the specification of the following targets, which can be the result of improved productivity:

- Developing software products in shorter periods of time;
- Developing software products in order to achieve a higher return on invest;
- Developing software products with higher quality.

The level of target achievement can be verified by the following key performance indicators:

- Productivity (related to software development as a production process and considering only work performance)

- Costs (considering personnel-, license- and infrastructure costs related to software development)
- Quality (referring to the developed software as a product)

Calculating costs should be established within the framework of the business administration processes of a company. Therefore, this chapter focuses on measuring the KPIs productivity and quality with appropriate methods.

Measuring productivity

The productivity of a production process is equivalent to its efficiency, which is calculated as output in relation to input:

$$\text{Productivity} \quad = \quad \frac{\text{Output}}{\text{Input}}$$

When looking at software development as a production process, output corresponds to the size of the produced software and the input to the production costs. In doing so, infrastructure costs can be neglected if the infrastructure already exists and can be used in new development processes without modification. Often open source tools are used for software development or enterprise licenses are available so that this cost factor can more or less be ignored. Thus, the input is reduced to personnel costs, in other words, the work performance necessary for the development:

$$\text{Productivity} \quad = \quad \frac{\text{Size}}{\text{Work Performance}}$$

In order to achieve that productivity measurements are comparable and can be used as reference values for indirect cost estimations of future development projects, the following requirements must be fulfilled:

- **System boundaries are precisely defined.**

  As an artefact of the production process, every product must be differentiated from its environment. If you measure the productivity of application software development, all components that are added after the development in a runtime environment, for example servers, operating systems, middleware, and so on, will be out of scope.

- **The process scope is consistent and precisely defined.**

  To compare measurements of different development processes, their beginning and end must be defined precisely. A simple way is to generally consider the overall development process, so that all phases and activities are included in the scope of the measurement. Isolated measurements of particular tasks as, for example, the requirements analysis, conceptualization, implementation, functional testing, and so on, require a precise separation of these phases, which in case of agile development is difficult or even impossible.

- **Processes finish with a consistent quality of results.**

  The development process considered by the measurement must finish with consistent quality defined as precisely as possible. In practice, it is helpful to specify a final quality gate, where checks and precise criteria are defined due to which the process can be considered as finished. Chapter "Anomaly #1: The impact of neglected analytical quality assurance" illustrates typical consequences if such criteria are not defined or met.

- **Input is measurable.**

  For productivity measurements, the considered input results from the personnel costs, in other words, the total work performance necessary for the process or project. Measurability requires this work performance to be determined precisely and reliably. Therefore it must be assured that no working time is considered where the employees have not actively contributed to the project. Furthermore, working time of employees who have serviced the project although they do not belong to the project team has to be included. This is often an organizational challenge.

- **Output is measurable.**

  Quantifying the output of a software development process, that is, the size of the software, requires a functional size metric such as, for example, the Function Point Analysis [ISO/IEC 20926 2009], the COSMIC method [COSMIC FSM 2014] or the Data Interaction Point method[PASS 2013].

  The first book of this series, entitled "Productivity and Performance Measurement – Measurability and Methods" [Luckhaus 2014], describes and compares such measurement methods. The empirical values published in this book have been measured using the Data Interaction Point method, but the conclusions thereof are valid for other metrics, as well as they comply with ISO/IEC 14143 [ISO/IEC 14143 2007]. The decision of PASS Consulting Group in favor of the Data Interaction Point method was determined by the following characteristics:

  - It is solely based on counting according to precisely defined rules - without estimations, approximations or even transformations of values by interval scales.

- Counting can be automated easily.
- It can be calibrated and thus be adapted to different types of software, for example, dialog-oriented web applications, legacy systems with character-based masks, transactional / real-time systems, and so on.

Measuring quality

In standard EN ISO 9000 quality is defined as "the degree to which a set of inherent characteristics meets requirements" [Kamiske/Brauer 2007]. In the context of a development process producing software on the basis of requirements, the concept of quality can be specified as the **degree of fulfilment of explicit and implicit requirements**. Explicit requirements are agreed on with a customer or product owner and documented comprehensibly. Implicit requirements can be understood as common expectations towards non-functional characteristics, that have not been explicitly agreed on or even been documented. An example for an implicit requirement is a "good" response-time behaviour of a system without "noticeable" waiting times – provided that maximum response times have not been explicitly described. Acceptable times vary from individual to individual – and thus the perception of quality. Therefore, it is better zu specifiy the expected response times quantitatively and thus measurably under different conditions. This way, an implicit requirement is transformed into an explicit requirement with the benefit, that it can be checked by measurements if it is met or not.

Considering software quality as the degree of fulfillment of all (explicit and implicit) requirements and also considering defects as not fulfilled requirements and therefore as quality deficits, it is obvious to use the **number of defects as a quality measure**. However, an important prerequisite is that multiple defects with the same implication, which, for example, have been identified by different testers, are counted only once. Furthermore, only those defects should be counted that are actually caused by non-fulfilled requirements, excluding handling errors or new requirements. An uncertainty of this approach is that defects are not differentiated and weighted due to their severity. A great advantage is that this method can be applied quite easily.

To compare the number of defects between different systems a measurement is required that includes the same time frame or test stage, for example, all production defects reported within one month. Furthermore, a difference in the size of the compared systems should be taken into account. If, for example, the same number of defects has been reported for two systems of the same age in one month, this can indicate a better quality of the system which the greater functional size. It is proven practice to weight the number of defects with the functional size of an application (according to the method used in, for example, data interaction points, function points or full function points). In the following context, this will be referred to as defect density:

$$\text{Defect Density} \quad = \quad \frac{\text{Number of Defects}}{\text{Size}}$$

Cycles of measurement, evaluation and optimization

The management model presented in this book is based on the cyclic application of measuring methods, the analysis and evaluation of their results and on the derived optimization methods. This approach creates transparency regarding performance differences, strengths as well as deficits of particular organizational units. It is useful to let an independent third party perform the measurements because such a transparency is often not in the interest of managers who are responsible for the development budgets: the performance and quality controlling. In addition to performing measurements, the following tasks should be under its responsibility:

- **Refining measuring methods.**

  The rules for counting and weighting must be clearly defined and justifiable. Thereby, the conformity with industry standards such as ISO/IEC 14143 is as important as the consideration of characteristics of the own system landscape. It might be helpful, for example, to weight the elements of character-based host masks and those of modern web-applications differently. Either way, the aim is that the measurement results correlate with the measured software characteristics, while the measurement is free from assessments and interpretive values.

- **Creating expertise on measuring methods.**

  The employees responsible for measuring, analysis and evaluation must have sufficient expertise in the utilized methods and the scientific background to ensure that the measuring results and the derived conclusions are not called into doubt.

- **Education and transparency.**

  Acceptance can only be reached if all employees working in software development understand the benefit of cyclic measurements and the measurement results. This not only requires an unconstrained way of dealing with the expert's knowledge. Measuring results must also be comprehensible, conclusions rationally explainable and reports understandable. These goals can be supported if measuring experts are generally available for questions and if training offers target all interested employees.

In this context, it is also necessary to clarify, whether measurements, as described above, allow conclusions to be drawn about the performance of individual employees or not. If, as described in this book, the input and output of the overall development process from business analysis up to handover for productive operation is measured, this results in the process performance, that is, the performance of the complete team involved in the process. Measuring the productivity of an individual employee requires the determination of his or her personal output, for example, the sum of all function points or data interaction points which have been developed by this person. Because commercial projects are characterized by a high level of team work and there are no components that have been developed completely and exclusively by only one individual, this is rather unrealistic.

II. Application of Measuring Methods

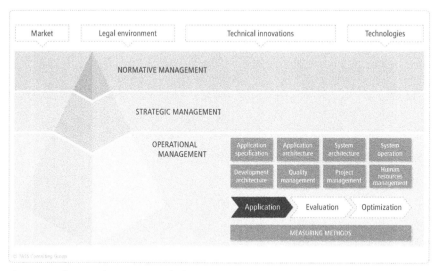

Figure 6: Application of measuring methods

This chapter illustrates some frequent applications of the measuring methods described earlier:

- For **completed development processes**: subsequent measures of different types of productivity.

- For **productive running systems**: the cyclic determination of quality indicators.

- For **planned development projects**: the pre-calculation of the effort – and subsequently: the project-accompanying iterative refinement of this estimation.

Measuring delivery- and new-development productivity

As the introduction has shown, standardization and reuse has the largest potential for increasing productivity. This becomes obvious when comparing delivery productivity and new-development productivity.

- **Delivery Productivity:**

  According to the productivity measuring method described in the previous chapter, the full functional size of the delivered application, including the reused components, serves as the output parameter. The total personnel costs up to the delivery must be determined as the input:

$$\text{Delivery Productivity} \ = \ \frac{\text{Delivered Functional Size}}{\text{Effort}}$$

  Generally, this type of productivity is more suitable for outward-looking comparisons, for example, which functional size the organization can deliver considering the necessary work effort.

- **New-development Productivity:**

  The size of the functionality, newly developed by the process, serves as the output. The total personnel costs up to the delivery must be determined as the input:

$$\text{New - development Productivity} \ = \ \frac{\text{Newly developed Functional Size}}{\text{Effort}}$$

The resulting productivity is more suitable for inward-looking comparisons regarding the performance of all production factors, in particular as an empirical value for future cost estimations of new-development projects.

If the delivered and the newly developed functional size is known, the degree of reusability can be calculated as follows:

$$\text{Degree of Reusability} = \frac{\text{Delivered Functional Size - Newly developed Functional Size}}{\text{Delivered Functional Size}}$$

Figure 7 is a case example showing KPIs of the development of a customer-specific travel management system. 90% of the delivered functional size could be realized by already existing, reused components. Only 10% had to be developed individually at the expense of 377 man days. Applying the formulas above results in a delivery productivity of 80.7 DIP/MD and a new-development productivity of 7.8 DIP/MD. If nothing had been reused so that the full functional size of 30,442 DIP would have had to be newly developed under the same conditions, expenses of 3,913 man days would have been the consequence – due to the measured new-development productivity of 7.8 DIP/MD (= 30,442 DIP / 7.8 DIP/MD). As the result of reusability, expenses of 3,536 man days were saved in this project.

Delivery productivity can reach very high values, if the effort moves towards zero (it increases exponentially with an effort reduction due to the quotient). In practice, the effort cannot reach zero because even in case of a reusability of 100%, effort for configuration and for final quality assurance is needed.

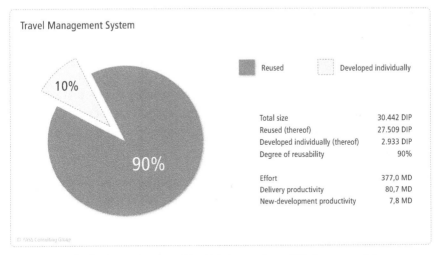

Figure 7: KPIs of a development project with a high degree of reusability (case example)

Measuring further-development productivity

When developing a new system the functional size is derived from the set of objects to be counted[1] – including or excluding reused components depending on the type of productivity. In case of further development, where the productivity of the development process for a new release or increment of an already existing application has to be determined, the relevant functional size not only includes new objects to be counted but also existing ones, as long as they are part of the considered development. Therefore, counting should consider the following types of objects:

---

1   Depending on the measuring method, objects to be counted can be, for example, data elements (DIP method), data movements (COSMIC method), elementary processes or logical files (Function Point Analysis).

- New objects, created by the development process
- Existing objects, modified by the development process
- Existing objects, that were deleted or deactivated

Rules, concerning the types of changes of already existing objects that are considered for counting must be clearly defined. Depending on the measuring method, these can be, for example, changes of the object properties or the use of objects by newly implemented functions.

Depending on the used method, the question may arise how to weight changed or deleted objects. In case of the Function Point Analysis and the Data Interaction Point method, it is proven practice to use the lowest weight in each category to count changed or deleted objects. When using Function Point, this would correspond to 3 for external input, 4 for external output, and so on. When using the DIP method it would generally be 1.

An important point is that changed objects to be counted only affect the further-development productivity and not the functional size of the application itself, which does not grow due to changes of, for example, data elements. The total functional size of the application after a further-development process amounts to the size it had before, plus the (method-compliant determined) size of new objects and minus the size of deleted objects.

In practice, the measuring effort often can be reduced through automated counting. Scripts can be created which count all objects – according to the used method - and thus determine the total functional size of the application on each run. The difference of its total size before and after a development process accounts for the size increase due to the process. If such a script or program additionally keeps an inventory of these objects, it can also identify objects which have been changed, used by the business logic or deleted since its last run.

Deriving quality indicators

In the chapter "measuring quality" the defect density has been described as a KPI of the quality of a system – in terms of meeting explicit and implicit requirements. Thus, the determination of this KPI requires measuring the number of defects and the functional size within the considered period.

In practice, the number of defects can often be retrieved from a ticketing system, where defect reports come in and can be categorized. The considered tickets should be filtered by a receipt date within the considered period because response and processing times are not relevant for a quality indicator used in the context of the described management model but correlations of the number of defects with, for example, particular events such as the production start of new releases or changes of basic conditions are. All defects should be counted where the root cause is a discrepancy from or non-fulfillment of (explicit or implicit) requirements. Not to be counted are handling errors, new requirements, inquiries, service requests or defects with a root cause which is outside the scope of the considered environment, for example operating infrastructure or external systems. Defects with the same root cause, which have been reported multiple times, should generally be counted only once.

Usually, the root cause of a received defect is not known immediately, but identified later in the course of a root cause analysis (RCA). Therefore, the number of defects initially retrieved for a new period must be considered as an approximation, which must be refined step-by-step. A root cause analysis method is decribed in the chapter "evaluation" later on.

The second value required as a quality indicator, in addition to the number of defects, is the functional size. Corresponding measurement methods have been described before in the context of measuring productivity. It should be considered that the size is not constant but usually increases with each development process. Thus, the size value always needs to be adjusted with regard to new or deleted objects – as described in the previous chapter "measuring further-development productivity".

Calculating the costs of planned development projects

An important utilization of empirical productivity values is the cost calculation of projects targeting new or futher development, which can be calculated easily by rearranging the known equation for productivity:

$$\text{Effort} \quad = \quad \frac{\text{Functional Size}}{\text{Productivity}}$$

This formula is the basis of the following five steps for calculating the personnel costs of a development project.

Step 1: Determining the size of functional requirements

For the methodical cost calculation based on measurements, detailed information about the software planned for development is needed. Utilizing a functional size measurement method such as the Funtion Point Analysis, the COSMIC method or the Data Interaction Point method requires detailed knowledge about the functional requirements, ideally, in the form of use cases and related data objects. Details of these methods are described in the first part of this book series with the title "Productivity and Performance Measurement – Measurability and Methods" (see chapter "book recommendations").

In the case of the functional requirements not being defined sufficiently, the accuracy should be estimated: At worst, how can the real value deviate upwards or downwards in percent? Be it 25% upwards and 25% downwards, the calculated development costs can also deviate by 25% in either direction in addition to the inaccuracy due to a difference between the used empirical productivity value and the real productivity of the development process.

Step 2: Finding an empirical value for the own productivity

Cost calculation based on measurements requires sound knowledge of the own productivity under different conditions. This is possible only if productivity is being measured frequently. The longer an organization performs these measurements and collects empirical values, the more accurate and reliable the derived cost calculation is.

In case of new development it is necessary to align all aspects affecting productivity. An empirical value should be selected where the following aspects of the related reference projects are as similar as possible to the planned one:

- Complexity of the business and technical issues, that is, the effort required to understand these issues
- Knowledge and experience of the team regarding the relevant business and technical issues
- The team's motivation, willingness to perform and ability to cooperate effectively
- The cooperation model of all stakeholders and providers, especially with respect to timelines and the quality of supplies and decisions
- Development paradigm, tools and architectures

- Degree of automation of development tasks (for example, as a result of model-driven software development and code generation), analytical quality assurance (for example, due to test automation) and build/ deploy processes
- Standards regarding processes, methods and policies (for example determining the required documentation or administrative tasks)

In case of the enhancement of an already existing system, where productivity measurements are performed regularly, finding the empirical value is simple. If no changes to the aforementioned aspects have been made since the last measurement of a large release or increment, this value is the best choice.

Step 3: Interpreting the result

If you enter the functional size determined in step 1 and the empirical productivity value identified in step 2 into the formula mentioned at the beginning of this chapter, the result is a value for the expected personnel costs, for example, in man days. This value can be understood as the effort for carrying out the same tasks that have been taken into account by measuring the productivity of the reference project. If the empirical value has been measured throughout the development process, starting from the analysis up to the hand-over to the production, the calculated result is equivalent to the effort for the same process steps.

Step 4: Identifying additional effort

When using a function-oriented size metric as described in step 1, non-functional requirements are disregarded. If projects have the scope of implementing functional requirements, the fullfilment of non-functional requirements is often a job of the system architecture and can be assured simply by configuration and scaling.

Thus, no implementation effort is required for an implementation of non-functional requirements, but possibly an effort for the quality assurance to verify that the used system architecture actually meets them. If the empirical productivity value determined in step 2 includes general quality assurance, it may not be necessary to consider this effort additionally. This depends on the extent of the required performance tests, security tests, and so on.

Sometimes procedural or organizational requirements can cause additional effort and should be estimated additionally, at least if they exceed the extent of the reference project and make up a sizeable part of the total development costs. Some examples are:

- Time-consuming coordination and interaction with external parties
- High effort for project management and controlling
- Additional documentation
- Travel time

Effort for knowledge building of the team, or rather, of the later users or administrators, insofar as it exceeds the extent considered by the reference project, may add on that.

Step 5: Identifying and mitigating risks

If the development effort has been calculated as described above, the accuracy of the calculation and thus the reliability of derived deadlines or offer prices should also be known. As early as in step 1, when determining the functional size, it must be clear how much this size value may deviate upwards or downwards due to imprecise or incomplete information. Additionally, there is an inaccuracy arising from the assumption that the planned development project has the same productivity as the reference project selected in step 2. On all accounts, the total inaccuracy must be considered a risk for derived deadlines, costs or budgets. If this risk is assessed as being high, an effective risk mitigation measure can be the juxtaposition of at least one alternative cost estimation method as, for example, the delphi method or an expert estimation.

If productivity measurements have been established for a while, the inaccuracy resulting from wrong empirical values of the own productivity (at step 2) is small compared to that resulting from incomplete or fuzzy functional requirements (at step 1). Thus, completing the requirements analysis and verifying the completeness and consistency of all requirements mitigates the initial uncertainty. If the functional size is then estimated again, the value of the expected development costs can be refined. The same is true for the milestones, when all concepts and specifications are completed and quality-assured. Under the condition of a careful conceptualization, the functional size estimated on this basis will improve the accuracy of the cost estimation even more.

III. Evaluation

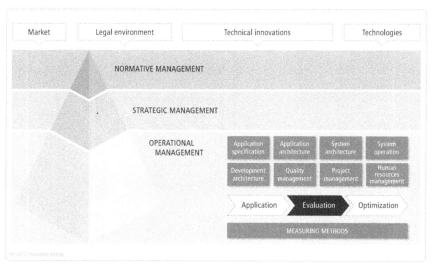

Figure 8: Evaluation of KPIs and root cause analysis

This chapter covers the evaluation of previously determined KPIs as well as a root cause analysis – as a prerequisite for purposeful improvements.

Analyzing the course of productivity over time

A first step in the evaluation of previously determined KPIs is the analysis of their time course. Usually, any continual deterioration is an indicator of underlying opportunities for saving time and costs and for quality improvements in the future. After the implementation of improvement measures, the development of the KPIs is an indicator for their effectiveness and sustainability.

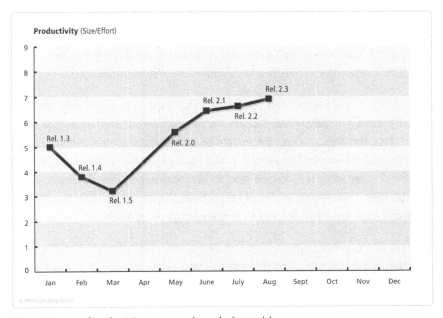

Figure 9: Course of productivity over several months (example)

Figure 9 shows the graphic representation of development productivity measured for every release of a sample system after the development process is completed and the release goes into production. The diagram clearly shows that, initially, productivity has decreased since the beginning of the year. In April and May a new major release was developed and went into production as release 2.0 in May, which included sustainable improvement measures.

It can often be observed that the accuracy of single measurements of the further development productivity is proportional to the size of the development: The smaller the functional size is, the more questionable is the measuring accuracy seems. The reason for this is that, in practice, the complexity implemented requirements often is very different, as the consideration of complexity by functional measurement methods is limited. These methods count data elements crossing the system boundaries as well as related structures in the database. In any case, a correlation between complexity and development costs is undisputed.

A good example is a small, new release of an application in which only some reports have been implemented. Reports are usually characterized by a large number of data elements crossing the system boundary and therefore being counted by functional measurement methods, which results in a large functional size. Let's assume that reporting data can be read by simple queries to the database, which requires little effort for the implementation. Both, the large functional size and the small development effort, lead to a calculated high productivity.

Another example is the implementation of a complex algorithm without user interaction, which then displays the result as one single value in a dialog field of the user interface. Because there is only one data element crossing the system boundary , applying a functional measurement method results in a low value of the implemented size. However, the implementation effort is high. Both, the small functional size and the high development effort, lead to a calculated low productivity.

When calculating the productivity of a small development scope, there is a risk that the complexity of the few implemented requirements is almost entirely higher or lower compared to the average and, therefore, the calculated productivity is not accurate – as shown in the examples above. These inaccuracies can be levelled by calculating the productivity of larger development scopes, where the requirements' complexity is evenly distributed. In practice, it has proven itself to summarize functional size and effort of all new releases of the last months in order to calculate the average further development productivity of a system:

$$\bar{P} \;=\; \frac{\Sigma\,\text{Functional Size}}{\Sigma\,\text{Effort}}$$

Productivity improvements or degradations become apparent if they are sustainable and have a perceptible value in relation to the total functional size. A good example for this is shown in table 2, which lists the fundamental values for the functional size S_n and the effort E_n for each new release as shown before in figure 9 in the course of productivity over time.

		S_n (DIP)	E_n (MD)	$\bar{P}$ (DIP/MD)
Rel 1.0	Okt	125	23	
Rel 1.1	Nov	23	2	
Rel 1.2	Dez	540	123	
Rel 1.3	Jan	125	15	5.0
Rel 1.4	Feb	410	149	3.8
Rel 1.5	Mrz	90	77	3.2
Rel 2.0	Mai	1,210	79	5.6
Rel 2.1	Jun	435	115	6.4
Rel 2.2	Jul	140	75	6.6
Rel 2.3	Aug	995	132	6.9

Table 2: Further development productivity by summarizing a period of four months (example)

In this example, the average productivity $\bar{P}$ is calculated by the sum of the functional size (in data interaction points) and the sum of the effort (in man days) of all releases developed in a period of four months. The average productivity in January, when release 1.3 is completed, is therefore calculated as follows:

$$\bar{P} = \frac{125 + 23 + 540 + 125}{23 + 2 + 123 + 15} = 5$$

Average productivity values calculated this way have proven to be resistant against outliers as can be seen, for example, in release 1.1 which would have a productivity of 11.5 in case of an individual consideration (results from a functional size of 23 DIP divided by an effort of 2 MD). Another outlier would be release 2.2 with an isolated measured productivity of 1.9 (results from a functional size of 140 DIP divided by an effort of 75 MD). Not until multiple individual measurements have been summarized, does the sustainability of the improvement become apparent, which was in effect since release 2.0. This is not detectable when looking at the time course of individual measurements only.

The period of 4 months for the summarization of further developments, which has been used in the example above, is sufficient to illustrate the mentioned effect of levelling the inaccuracies of smaller development scopes. Depending on the release cycles, different periods such as a complete year ($n = 12$) can be useful.

Internal benchmarks

In addition to the informative value of a single system's course of productivity, the comparison of different systems or organizational units can be useful, as figure 10 shows.

The basis for the comparability of values measured with different systems is their independence from technical characteristics and the orientation of the measurement methods towards use cases. This is generally given in case of functional measurement methods as the Function Point Analysis, the COSMIC method and

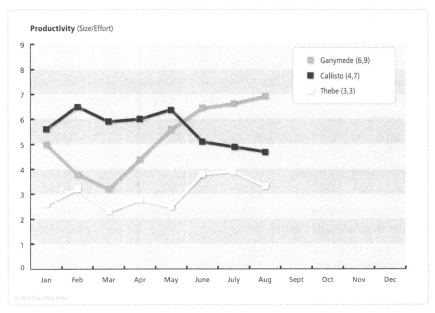

Figure 10: Internal productivity benchmark (example)

the Data Interaction Point method. Comparisons of systems or IT shops of the same organization, also called internal benchmarks in particular, help to identify the most productive teams or organizational units, also called „the best in class", others can learn from. This requires an analysis of their success factors and a check of the transferability to other teams or shops. If an organization is able to promote an internal improvement competition based on transparency and openness for their valid measurements and without assigning blame or punishments, this will result in high planning and scheduling reliability perceivable by the market, as well as in additional cost reduction effects.

External benchmarks

External benchmarks compare values measured in own projects or shops with those of other companies, thus helping to realize the own performance indicators' market adequacy. However, this requires the comparability of the used measurement methods and their underlying conditions. Even in the case of widespread methods such as the Function Point Analysis, this is problematic, because many publications show productivity values without the underlying conditions such as, for example, development duration, system type or technology (dialog-oriented, web or mainframe, transactional/ real-time, and so on), the scope of the considered development process, industry, team size, year of development, and so on. This makes an interpretation of the discrepancies towards the own values difficult. Besides that, it is often not clear if a certain version of a measurement method or an approximation method was used. This significantly reduces the usability of measurements for external benchmarks.

Reference values

The interpretation of measured values requires guidance by a reference or base value. One concept is to use a fixed target value and to visualize the differences of the considered systems from this target value or the time course of their convergences or divergences. Another concept is to use the average of the overall organization at each measurement point and to visualize the differences of the considered systems within the benchmark compared to the average as well as to the time course of the average value.

If a reference value for benchmarks is set as a fixed target value by the management, this value should not only reflect the productivity of the organization, which is needed for competitiveness. It should also be a value which is realistically achievable within a defined period of time and which should require an improvement even of „the best in class".

If a company decides on the dynamic version of the reference value, it is preferable to calculate it by using the average of all productivity measurements of the considered systems over the last months which equates to Pk:

$$\bar{P} = \frac{\sum_{k=1}^{n} P_k}{n}$$

Figure 11 shows a sample benchmark of three systems, calculated in August of the respective year, where the reference value is calculated from the average of all measurements from January to August:

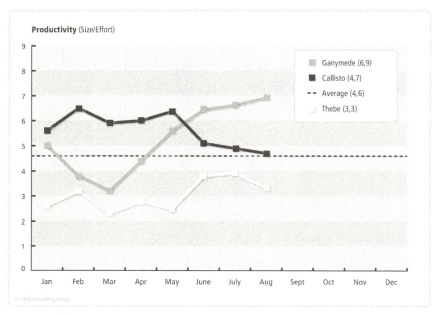

Figure 11: Reference value derived from the average of all measurements from January to August (example)

The legend of the diagram shows the productivity as measured in August and arranges the systems according to their relation to the average as a reference value. This diagram provides the following information at a glance:

- **Current productivity values**, which are required for the calculation of the development effort for future releases of the considered systems.
- **Development of productivity values over time.** If the productivity of a particular system decreases for months, a root cause analysis is recommendable to identify control measures which are suited to reverse this

trend. If the productivity of a particular system increases significantly, a root cause analysis may also be worthwhile to review their transferability to other systems.

- **Systems whose productivity is below average.** As „worst in class" these must be urged to actively perform efficient improvement measures.

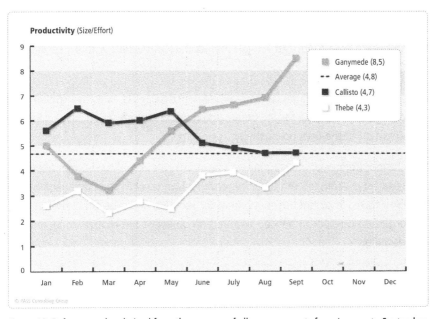

Figure 12: Reference value derived from the average of all measurements from January to September (example)

If particular systems succeed in improving their performance indicators, this also results in an improvement of the average as a reference value. In other words: it sets the bar higher. This becomes clear when comparing the examples shown in figures 11 and 12. Figure 11 shows the productivity values measured in August of the according year. The average lies at 4.6, and the systems Ganymede and Callisto show an above average productivity in this month. Figure 12 shows the values measured in September. Due to improvements of the systems Ganymede and Thebe, the average increases to 4.8. Even though the productivity of Callisto has not changed, it is hence below the average now. Through the dynamics of this approach no system can rely on maintaining a position without continuous improvements.

Another benefit of averages as dynamic reference values is, that they can be used as aggregated indicators for the organization under consideration, visualizing the development of the own productivity.

Conclusion: Reference values play an important role in KPI-based management. They can serve as an orientation in regard to a target set by the management and required to reach competitiveness. Another function could be the monitoring of the organization's performance – without an objective but motivated by internal competition.

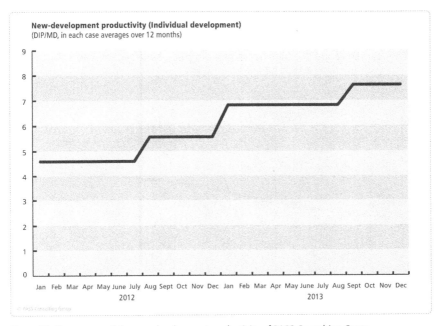

Figure 13: Time course of the new development productivity of PASS Consulting Group

Comparing quality with productivity

In light of past experience, there is an impact of a system's quality to its further development productivity. Therefore, it is crucial to compare productivity measurements and benchmarks with quality indicators. An important requirement for the validity of this comparison is that the calculation of the further-development productivity also considers the effort for defect analyses and bug fixes spent during the development process of the considered release (see chapter II, „Measuring further-development productivity").

A convenient way to compare productivity and quality is to show the quality indicator, described as defect density in chapter "Measuring quality", together with the time course of the productivity in one diagram, as shown in figure 14.

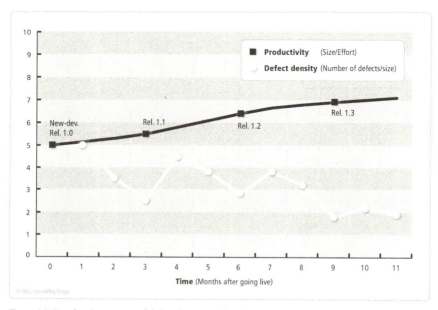

Figure 14: Regular time course of defect density and productivity (example)

Figure 14 shows the usual normal case, or ideal case, which is characterized by the following properties:

- The defect density decreases over a longer period of time. Experience shows that it initially increases slightly after the launch of a new release due to undetected defects, but then continues to decrease.

- The productivity of release (increment) 1.1 more or less corresponds to the new development productivity of release 1.0, and improves continuously because less and less defects need to be fixed and quality improves, which has an additional, positive influence on maintainability.

Such a time course is representative of systems which completed a new development process with good quality before going live.

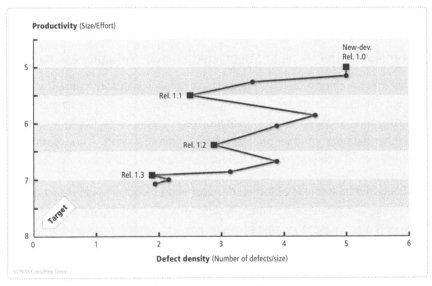

Figure 15: Regular time course of defect density and productivity in a XY diagram (example)

A different way of visualizing the time course of productivity and defect density is using an XY diagram where the axes are scaled in such a way that 'better' values lead to the lower left corner of the diagram. This two-dimensional view enables a better orientation and informs whether the further development of a system is moving in the right direction, towards the origin of the coordinate system, or not. Figure 15 shows the normal case or ideal case as described before, using this two-dimensional view. It clearly shows that, monitored over a longer period of time, or rather on the way from release 1.0 via releases 1.1 and 1.2 to release 1.3, it is going in the right direction.

Sometimes, the following patterns can be encountered which are reliable indications of neglected analytical quality assurance or technical debts.

Anomaly #1: The impact of neglected analytical quality assurance

Sometimes development projects neglect their analytical quality assurance and go live with an insufficiently tested system. The reason for this may be time pressure. At first glance, a positive effect of such projects is the high productivity, which may be higher than that of other projects with a higher test effort. A drawback is the inherent risk of errors which is typical for systems with insufficient test coverage.

Probably, the time course of further development productivity and defect density will be similar to the visualizations in figures 16 and 17. After going live, the defect density is often higher than that of similar projects, but it decreases with ongoing bug-fixing. The further-development productivity (from release 1.1) is significantly worse than that of the productivity measured for the new development of release 1.0, due to the impact of the effort for bug-fixes. After the consequences of the neglected, analytical quality assurance have largely been caught up, the direction aimed for is on track again – in other words: the productivity increases and the defect density decreases.

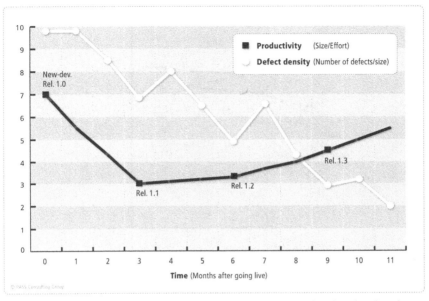

Figure 16: Regular time course of defect density and productivity in case of neglected analytical QA (example)

Measurements of the test coverage, performed during the new development process, can serve as early indicators of such an anomaly. There are various tools such as Cobertura [GitHub 2015] or JaCoCo [Mountainminds 2015], which can be used for these measurements. Generally, low test coverage increases the risk of production defects, resulting in an added effort for analyses and bug-fixes.

This approach shifts the test effort from a development project to the users of a productive system. As a consequence, this effort is not included in the project's cost accounting, which increases its (initial) productivity. However, experience shows that over a longer period of time, the total costs for the less productive

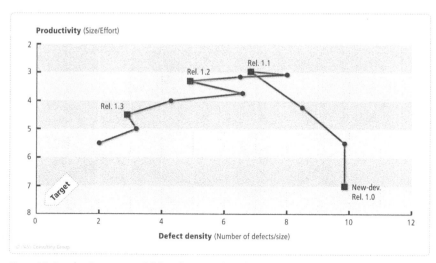

Figure 17: Regular time course of defect density and productivity in case of neglected analytical QA shown in a XY diagram (example)

further-development and bug-fixes are higher than it would be the case if the new development process had been completed with appropriate test coverage and bug-fixes prior to the go-live. Conclusion: **Quality has its price. Bad quality has an even higher price.**

Anomaly #2: The impact of technical debts

Technical debts are a metaphor for productivity increases by negligence, that go beyond the neglected, analytical quality assurance described above. Possible causes are time pressure, lack of experience and/or know-how deficits. The problem of these debts is that they must be borne by the employees responsible for maintenance and further development of a system – apart from the high interest that has to be repaid over a long period of time. Interestrates are a metaphor for a significantly worse further development productivity, resulting in higher costs.

Some measures for increasing the productivity of the development process for a new system, at the expense of a sustained limitation of its maintainability, are:

- Incomplete implementation of non-functional requirements
- Postponed fixing of known errors
- Neglecting the technical design
- Repeated implementation of similar or identical functionality (in contrast to generic programming or reuse)
- Neglecting the structuring and commenting code as well as its robustness and an appropriate error handling
- Insufficient documentation
- Processes or infrastructures, that are non existing, immature or too complex for version control, configuration management, build and deployment

It is a clear indicator for technical debt if the further-development productivity is significantly lower than the value of the new development – and if it deteriorates from release to release. Thereby, the defect density can be inconspicuous because problems are more likely to occur in maintainability than in functional correctness (examples: figures 18 and 19).

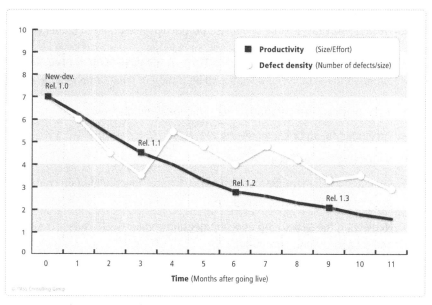

Figure 18: Regular time course of defect density and productivity in case of technical debt (example)

The XY diagram (figure 19) clearly shows that a system which has been put into productive operation burdened with technical debt does not converge to the preferred direction (increasing productivity by decreasing defect density). Instead, it to derivate with each new release. In contrast to anomaly #1, where analytical quality assurance is neglected during the development process and delayed until production, technical debt usually cannot be mended by making an acceptable, correctional effort. In most cases, a time-consuming redesign or refactoring of the whole system is required.

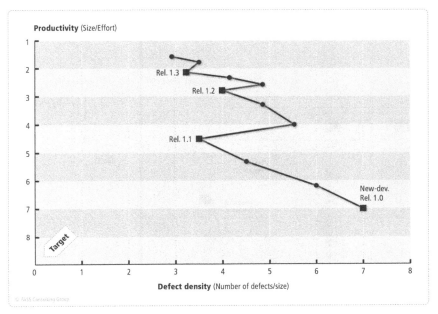

Figure 19: Regular time course of defect density and productivity in case of technical debt shown in a XY diagram (example)

In addition to the analysis of the productivity course, frequent code analyses can provide early indices of technical debt and thus of limited maintainability. They can be automatically performed by tools such as, for example, SonarQube [Sonar-Source 2014] and should be complemented by manual reviews. Depending on the programming language, SonarQube is able to check for key words such as TODO or FIXME, and measure comment density, complexity, cohesion or coupling. It can detect known error patterns within the code so that some defects can be found prior to functional testing, that is, immediately after coding. It is proven practice to integrate SonarQube into a build process as early as possible, configured as a nightly build or a continuous integration, thus giving developers as well as quaility managers feedback about the code quality practically in realtime.

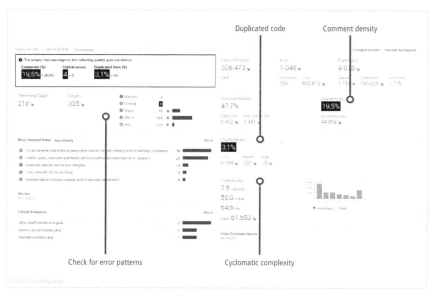

Figure 20: Summary of the results of a code analysis by SonarQube (example)

Root cause analyses

Many defects bear the potential to pay up the costs of their analysis and correction in multiples. At first, a root cause analysis seems like an additional expense compared to a quick bugfix, but actually, it is a measure to save effort which otherwise would have to be spent for the handling of related defects in the future. Thus, root cause analyses sustainably improve productivity and quality.

In practice it is required to find the real cause, that is, the onset of the cause-and-effect chain, of each defect first. This is usually not a superficial cause such as a 'programming error'. It has paid off to proceed by applying the 5-Why method [Sondalini 2005] by asking the question „Why" several times. Once the cause-and-effect chain has been traced back so far, that no useful answer to the 'Why?' can be found anymore, the root cause of the defect has probaly been found thus leading us to an effective improvement measure. The error message which says that the user cannot change the content of a specific field of a mask, although his role should enable him to do so, may serve an example:

Question	Answer
Why can the field content not be edited by a specific user?	It is a read-only field for him/her.
Why is it read-only?	The user's role does not have the appropriate right.
Why is the user's role missing this right?	Because it has not been assigned when setting-up the user roles.
Why has it not been assigned?	It was not included in the specification of the user roles

Table 3: Example for a root cause analysis inspired by the 5-Why method

Obviously, it could be further questioned why the specification of the user roles was incomplete. By no means is it a 'programming error' or 'GUI error', but rather an 'incorrect specification', possibly even a new requirement (and thus no error at all). Possible measures to prevent future errors of the category 'incorrect specification' are: more accuracy in requirements management and specification, appropriate quality assurance and an approval process for the specification prior to its implementation.

For the practical application of root cause analyses it can be recommended to standardize the error causes company-wide and to ensure that only root causes from this schema are selected. Technically this can be done by a picklist in the applied ticketing system or an error tracking tool. Standardization is crucial for easy evaluations of the frequency of errors with regard to the root cause category. These show in which areas improvement measures are probably the most effective – due to the related number of errors. In reference to the above mentioned example: If 25% of all detected errors were to be assigned to the category 'specification wrong', it should be clear for those responsible that they have a problem with the creation and quality assurance of specifications. But, in other words, they also have the chance to improve their error rate by 25% with only a few targeted measures and save high costs for bugfixing.

In the management model introduced in this book the root cause analysis is part of the phase evaluation, whose results provide a basis for the phase optimization. It is proven practice to group the schema of standardized error causes at top level according to the areas of activity, the so called key performance areas (KPAs), for the subsequent optimization as illustrated in figure 21.

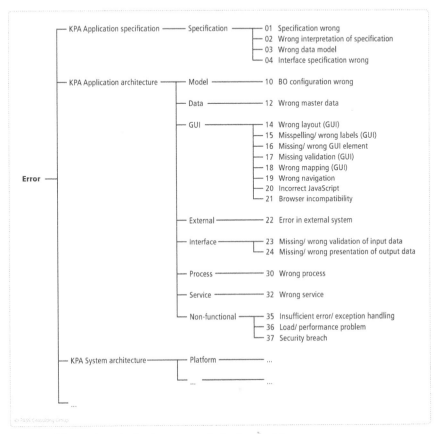

Figure 21: Schema of standardized error causes (extract, example)

IV. Optimization

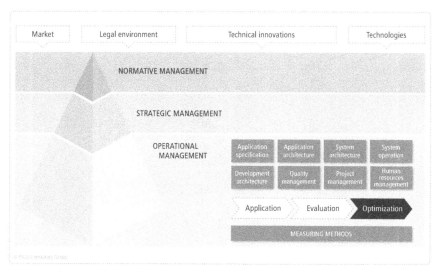

Figure 22: Planning and implementing improvement measures

After indicators have been derived and evaluated and root causes have been analyzed, the cycle of the management model is completed by the planning and implementation of improvement measures.

Key Performance Areas

Figure 23 shows some so called key performance areas (KPAs). These are areas that impact on the management model's KPIs, namely productivity, costs and quality, and represent fields for possible improvements. The color of each intersection between a KPA and a KPI is an indicator of the empirical improvement effect on the KPI, which can be caused by a measure in the KPA. In this context the term empirical effect means that different conditions can lead to different improvement effects.

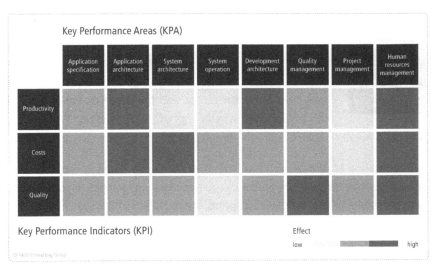

Figure 23: Impact of different KPAs on KPIs (empirical values)

If a KPI indicates a 'bad' value, measures within these KPAs with a strong improvement effect should be searched for first. The following chapters briefly outline some proven measures for each KPA. A more detailed look at all success factors, details and experiences would go beyond the scope of this book. For this purpose, this book series will be continued and further releases will focus on the optimization of specific KPAs on the basis of practical experiences.

Application specification

An indicator for problems in this area is a conspicuous frequency of errors, where an analysis generally results in a root cause related to the application specification. Depending on the granularity of the error causes and the depth of the analysis, it can be apparent whether specification faults or simply fuzzy descriptions, which have been misinterpreted by the developers, are the problem.

Furthermore, a high number of late, new requirements (change requests) is a strong indicator for problems with the requirements management, in other words, with the identification, precise description, consideration of the specification and traceability of requirements.

Effective improvement measures can be found in the area of development standards, for example, as process models: guidelines on how requirements should be described and specifications should be created, checks for precision and completeness, the involvement of customers and product owners, and so on.

Influence on KPIs:

- **Productivity**: Medium. During the development process, incomplete or fuzzy specifications can cause additional costs for callbacks or reworks. The costs for fixing defects during the specification phase are significantly lower than at a later stage, when error analyses, code changes and retests are required or patches or new releases need to be installed in the production environment.

- **Costs**: Medium, for the reasons mentioned above.

- **Quality**: Medium, because many defects can be avoided and are neither found nor reported by users.

Application architecture

Application architecture

If the evaluation of root cause analyses leads to a conspicuous frequency of errors related to the application architecture, this can be an indicator of fundamental problems in this area. Experience has shown that most errors have their origin in this area. For this reason, the related error causes should be further divided into groups as, for example, processes, functions, database, interfaces or the GUI, allowing more precise conclusions.

As described in the previous chapter, a code analysis can provide more indicators, for example, measures of the cohesion of methods, the coupling or the percentage of redundant code.

Effective improvement measures are development standards such as, for example, frameworks and standard architectures, but particularly reuse. The less individually, implemented code, the less development effort and risk of coding errors.

Influence on KPIs:

- **Productivity**: High, because due to a high degree of reusability the development effort can be reduced significantly (see the example given in the introduction).
- **Costs**: High, likewise because of the strong lever to reduce the development effort.
- **Quality**: Medium. Usually, reused components are proven and quality assured – in contrast to individual implementations.

System architecture

With an appropriate definition of error causes, a root cause analysis can provide indices for problems related to the system architecture, for example, in case of deficiencies with availability, load behavior or information security. Further source of indices for problems within this KPA is the monitoring of the system operation.

Good risk mitigation measures are proven standard architectures which meet the requirements as well as the compliance with industry standards such as, for example, ISO/IEC 27001, BSI basic protection or PCI DSS.

Influence on KPIs:

- **Productivity**: Low, because development/ application architecture and system architecture are usually decoupled. Due to a persistence layer, for example, the implemented business logic is independent of the database management system. In other words: changes of the system architecture should not cause high implementation efforts within the application.

- **Costs**: High, due to the impact of license costs, which lie within the range of expensive license models of established technology providers, and open source software without payment obligations towards a licensor.

- **Quality**: Medium. Issues of the system architecture can strongly impact on non-functional requirements, for example, in the area of availability, load behavior or information security.

System operation

Indicators for problems in the area of system operation are system failures affected by users, operational restrictions as well as the impact of attacks which cannot be prevented by the system architecture (by firewalls, intrusion prevention systems, encryption, load balancing, and so on).

A very effective mitigation measure is the strict compliance with proven industry standards such as, for example, ISO 22301 for business continuity or the information security standards ISO/IEC 27001, BSI basic protection and PCI DSS.

Influence on KPIs:

- **Productivity**: Low, if considering software development productivity, because development/ application architecture and system architecture are usually decoupled. An exception is the support of the system's logging and monitoring facilities by an implemented functionality of the operated application which can cause implementation effort.

- **Costs**: Medium, due to the resource consumption of the data centers and, depending on the agreed system availability, a synchronized operation of redundant components or even data centers.

- **Quality**: Low, but not without impact because to meet some non-functional requirements as, for example, availability requirements or information security, also depends on the system operation.

Development architecture

A long-term low value of the development productivity is an indicator of potential problems within the development architecture, that is, with the technologies, methodologies, methods, tools used for software development.

Proven mitigation measures are development standards such as, for example, programming guidelines, design patterns, development environments that can be integrated with version control systems, code analysis tools, or even development frameworks with reusable technical components. Automation approaches such as model-driven development are more effective: business processes are executed or code is being generated, based on abstract models. Further examples with automation potential are the continuous integration (build automation), code analyses and the execution of test cases.

Influence on KPIs:

- **Productivity**: High, because especially automation approaches in the area of development processes can reduce the effort significantly.

- **Costs**: Medium. Reducing the development effort by automation often go hand in hand with additional effort for the development, introduction and training of standards and automation technology and is sometimes complemented by license costs.

- **Quality**: Medium. The risk of errors is lower if processes are executed automatically and not manually. A good example is code generation, where the quality of generated code can be controlled by a template and is therefore consistent. In contrast, the quality of individually implemented code depends on numerous factors, is heterogeneous and hard to control.

Quality management

A defect density that is permanently above average and an accumulation of issues where defects, which have already been reported as fixed, must be reopened after retesting, are a clear indication of deficits in quality management.

In quality management, a distinction is made between constructive, organizational and analytical quality assurance. **Constructive quality assurance** includes measures to prevent errors. Such measures can be related to standards, methods and tools for performing quality control at the earliest possible stage, moreover to the knowledge and experience of the involved people, to compliance with proven standards or automating tasks which have previously been done manually.

The aim of **organizational quality assurance** is to support quality with the help of expert roles and panels, which contribute their knowledge and experience to the development process, advise the development team and check and approve their artifacts. These can be, for example, business or technical committees, security experts, specialists for topics such as architecture, data modeling, user experience or test automation, controlling boards or even a steering committee.

While constructive as well as organizational quality assurance both have the aim to prevent errors, **analytical quality assurance** is responsible for existing errors. Its task is to use reviews to prove conformity with the requirements, the preparation of tests (creating test cases, test data and test environments) and the test execution.

Influence on KPIs:

- **Productivity**: Medium. Manually performed measures of analytical quality assurance lead to high expenses and decrease productivity. This effort
  can be saved and productivity increased temporarily by neglecting the
  analytical quality assurance, however the impacts are higher error costs
  and lower productivity of the further development. Generally, with quality
  assurance at the earliest stage of a development process, bug-fixing is less
  expensive than at later stages. Test automation can reduce the effort for
  test execution. Thus, both measures have the effect of increasing productivity.

- **Costs**: Medium, because the cost drivers mentioned before (manually
  performed QA measures, late error detection) are also drivers of personnel
  costs. In addition, costs caused by the effects of unfixed bugs, in particular
  operational disturbances, limited usability or the impact on downstream
  processes or systems, can hardly be quantified. Moreover, costs can incur
  for tools supporting the analytical quality assurance.

- **Quality**: High, due to the direct impact of all described measures on the
  error rate.

Project management

The repeated postponement of planned and agreed milestones is a solid indicator of problems in the area of project and
risk management. This can be visualized early on with the help
of a milestone trend analysis. Other indices are negligences
in reviewing quality criteria, for example, if specifications are
implemented before they have been reviewed and approved, or if new releases or
increments go live before they have been tested sufficiently.

This area can be improved by sharing models such as a project management office (PMO), which is a cross-divisional organizational unit, bundling competencies and supporting multiple projects with project management services. Furthermore, it is recommendable to align team size and methods of project management with the size of the project. From experience, the need for project management services correlates with the developed size, not necessarily with the delivered size. In case of a high degree of reusability and a low share of individual implementation, the need for project management is fairly low.

Influence on KPIs:

- **Productivity**: Low, but not without impact. Especially project management services not adapted to the project size can cause disproportionately high personnel costs and thus reduce productivity. On the other side, performing project management ensures the compliance with agreed milestones, budgets and quality criteria and anticipates project risks, thus avoiding additional expenses.
- **Costs**: Low, for the reasons explained above.
- **Quality**: Medium, because project management is also responsible for compliance with the agreed quality criteria and for performing all planned measures of analytical quality assurance.

Human resources management

For this key performance area, there is no unambiguous indicator. Lack of experience, insufficient knowledge or low motivation of the assigned employees can cause all kinds of problems. Conducting a project assessment from a different perspective, that is, letting employees perform it who are not directly involved in the development processes, can be helpful.

This key performance area is the only one with a strong impact on all KPIs. One reason for this is the fact that software development is knowledge work, that requires knowledge about the relevant business and technical topics in order to be successful. Improvement measures in human resources can be achieved by chosing employees with a sound knowledge base or by investing in the establishment of a furture knowledge pool in human resources development. An additional success criteria is knowledge management, that is, the ability to give the right person access to the required knowledge at the right time.

In addition to the particular characteristics of individuals, their ability to work in a team has a huge impact. Complex tasks can frequently be solved faster by using methods such as pair programming or pair testing, where two employees complement each other and are more productive as a team. However, this requires a management that supports team work as well as team-minded employees. Further success criteria are sharing knowledge and a collective responsibility for the quality of artefacts. Experience shows that performance differences between employees, which can be measured up to a factor of 30, become less important if the overall team performance is much higher than the total sum of the individual performances. Important prerequisites are an initial team-building process accompanied by team development measures. The performance of the German team during the Soccer World Cup 2014 serves as a good example, which was not the result of individual performances but of excellent teambuilding.

Influence on KPIs:

- **Productivity**: High.
- **Costs**: High.
- **Quality**: High.

Calculating the effectiveness of improvement measures

Each improvement measure requires effort, which must be evaluated in relation to the potential benefits, in particular to the expected productivity increase and the resultant cost savings. The leverage effect of KPAs on KPIs, as shown on a three-step scale in figure 23, provides a rough orientation on how in some areas improvement measures can be more effective than in others. In addition, this chapter provides a method for the analytical determination of the total degree of efficiency after one or more measures have been implemented.

The range or coverage of each improvement measure plays a significant role, that is, to which extent is the total development process being affected by the respective measure. Figure 24 gives an example: A measure doubling the productivity of a sub process, which accounts for one half of the total effort (dark bar), only increases the total productivity of the overall development process by a third (33%). The explanation is that productivity and effort are reciprocal, that is, an increase in productivity leads to a reduction of the effort – and vice versa. The improvement measure illustrated in figure 24 results in a 50 percent decrease of the effort for 50 percent of the total work – in total a reduction of the effort by 25 percent (by a quarter, 1/4). Due to the reciprocity the remaining three quarters (3/4) of the original work equate to four thirds (4/3) of the original productivity. This is an increase of a third (1/3, 33%).

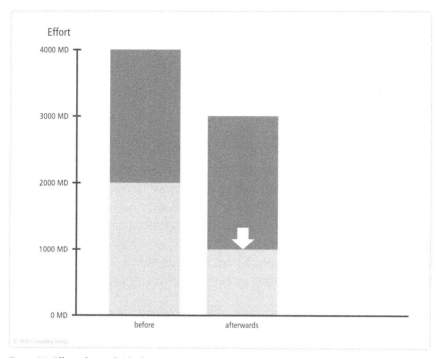

Figure 24: Effect of an individual improvement measure (example)

In order to assess the effective productivity improvement of various measures, it is important to know if these measures influence each other. As long as they are independent, the total productivity can be determined easily by calculating the reduction of the effort for each measure and putting it in relation to its coverage of the total process (percentage of total work). This results in the remaining total effort and thus in the total effective productivity increase. Figure 25 shows two measures, each of which improves the productivity independently by 100% and covers complementary sub-processes by one quarter of the total work. The resulting effort of both methods corresponds to three quarters (3/4, 75%) of the original effort in total, thus the resulting productivity is four thirds (4/3), amounting to an increase of a third (1/3, 33%).

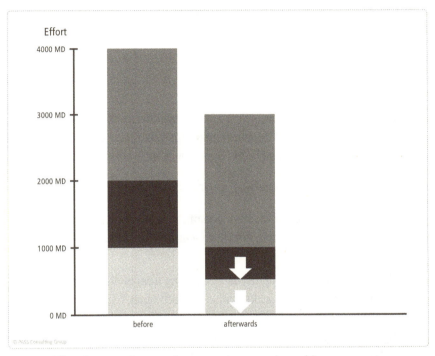

Figure 25: Effect of two complementary improvement measures (example)

These examples show that not alone is the effectiveness of selective improvements crucial, but also their attributed coverage of the development process.

If improvement measures cover identical sub-processes, their effort reduction factors can be multiplied to receive the total reduction. Assuming that both measures of the previous example are not effective in different but entirely in the same sub-processes, an improvement as illustrated in figure 26 is the result. The remaining effort of the sub-process can be calculated as 50% * 50% = 25% (one quarter). Before implementation of the measures, this sub-process covered 25% of the total work, therefore, the remaining effort is 13/16 in total.

$$\frac{3}{4} + \frac{1}{4} \cdot \frac{1}{4} = \frac{3}{4} + \frac{1}{16} = \frac{13}{16}$$

In other words, productivity has increased by sixteen thirteenth (16/13) or by 23% (3/13) of the original value. If complementary sub-processes were to be covered, as shown in the previous example, the productivity increase would be 33%.

These examples lead to the following important conclusions:

- The higher the range or the coverage of the total development process (regarding work), the more effective measures for productivity improvements will be.

- The total productivity improvement resulting from multiple measures depends on how these measures influence each other. Usually, the resulting effectiveness correlates with the degree of independency, which is hard to figure out in practice. At most, the expected degree of improvement can be determined within a certain interval.

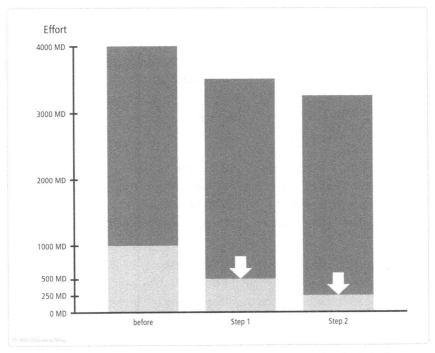

Figure 26: Impact of two improvement measures consecutively implemented in identical sub-processes (example)

Adjusting and calibrating measuring methods

In addition to improvement measures in the action areas described before, it can become necessary to optimize the measuring methods. However, changes of a measuring method usually lead to a non-comparability of future measured values with those measured before the change. Hence, each organization should hesitante to implement such changes. Reasons for changes at the basis of the management model can be:

- Frequently, there is a noticeable difference between the cost estimation performed before or at the beginning of the development process and the actual costs – even if many empirical values of the own productivity are available (see chapter 'Calculating the costs of planned development projects').

- The productivity measured for the further development of particular systems differs significantly from the reference value over a longer period of time - and no other reason than inaccuracies of the measuring method can be found.

In these cases the following changes may be helpful:

- Refining the rules, that is, deciding which software characteristics or system components lie within the scope for determining the development size – and which do not. This can, for example, become necessary if components developed once are henceforth reused and thus provide functionality, which need not to be implemented individually.

- The consideration of additional functional users which interact with the system. These can be, for example, new input or output devices such as sensors or cyber-physical systems (devices enriched with IT) – in addition to the traditional masks and graphical user interfaces.

- Changes of the weights of the objects to be counted, which are better suited for the interactional complexity. An example is the difference between character-based masks of a mainframe application and the dialogs of a state-of-the-art web application.

Generally, the effectiveness of adjusting and calibrating the measuring methods should be checked subsequently. In case of insufficient improvements of the measurement accuracy, the adjustment and calibration should be repeated.

V. Conclusion

Improving productivity is a desirable objective. It leads to the development of software in less time and in higher quality, and it achieves a higher return on investment. However, we cannot perceive productivity with our physical senses, and a limited consideration of mere costs – the so-called management of consumption – is not suitable for providing the necessary information directed towards the future.

The productivity of a development process must be calculated specifically. These calculations not only include the process costs (personnel costs) but also the development size, whose determination requires a suitable measuring method. Due to the dependencies, any analytical view on productivity requires the simultaneous measurement of quality – and thus a further measuring method. Finally, license and infrastructure costs should be considered as well as process or personnel costs. Hence, three key performance indicators (KPIs) – productivity, costs and quality – are required for a sustainable performance improvement.

With the help of these KPIs an organization can identify performance differences and can find out whether planned or unplanned changes lead to an improvement or deterioration and to what extent. In this context, single measurements alone cannot lead to success. It is crucial to analyse these KPIs in their temporal course. The management model introduced in this book, in use and proven for several years now by the PASS Consulting Group, is based on the cyclic determination and evaluation of these KPIs and their optimization measures in different key performance areas (KPAs). Thereby, all measures are selected by considering cost / benefit aspects, which are based on empirical values of the leverage effect specific KPAs have on the KPIs, as well as on calculations of the achievable productivity improvements.

The consistent application of this management model verifiably results in pro-ductivity improvements. The only disadvantage could be that an organization considers to be satisfied with small steps of improvement, and subsequently over-looking the potential of paradigm changes that would enable major and larger improvements as shown in the introduction of this book on the basis of empirical projects.

Glossary

Actor

User or external system interacting with a target system in the context of a →use case.

Agile Development

Type of development characterized by →incremental development, improvements achieved by learning of individuals as well as of the organization, and a close collaboration between all related parties.

Algorithm

Finite sequence of executable instructions to solve a problem.

Algorithmic Complexity

Complexity of the program logic implemented in an application.

Application Architecture

Also: Application design, software architecture or software design. Definition of an application's internal construction by components, their responsibilities, interfaces and communication.

Base Functional Component

Also: BFC. Step of a →Use case. According to →ISO/IEC 14143, BFCs are the basis of the →Functional size measurement.

Baseline

In project management, the initial plan used for measuring the project progress. In IT controlling, the reference value in a →benchmark.

Benchmark

Comparative analysis of metrics or processes with a target value (also: →baseline) or with a reference process.

Cloud

Also: Cloud computing. →Virtualization of IT infra-structure and its provision via the internet.

Code Metric

Method for measuring the software size on the basis of characteristics of the source code.

Complexity

In software development complexity means the effort required to understand a program or →algorithm.

Component

Capsulated and reusable software unit providing services via well-defined interfaces which can be combined and executed unchanged with other components.

Continuous Improvement Process

A process of steady, small steps of improvement. In IT, this means a repetitive cycle of the identification of potential improvements on the basis of →root cause analyses and →benchmarks, the respective planning, implementation and a check of the effectiveness.

COSMIC

Common Software Measurement International Consortium, an international grouping of software measurement experts with the objective of promoting and disseminating the →COSMIC method.

COSMIC Method

Also: →Full Function Points Method. Method for measuring the size of software by counting data movements related to →use cases. Standardized by the norm →ISO/IEC 19761.

Cyclomatic Complexity

Also: McCabe metric. →Complexity of a concrete implementation, based on the number of independent branches of the program flowchart. Developed in 1976 by Thomas J. McCabe.

Data Interaction Point Method

Also: DIP method. Method for measuring the size of software by counting interactions between →actors and a considered system related to →use cases.

Defect

Also: Bug. Nonfulfillment of or non-compliance with an →explicit or →implicit requirement.

Defect Density

Indicator of a system's →quality. Calculated from the number of →defects in a particular time range in relation to the system's size.

Delivery Productivity

→Productivity related to the effective size of a system as delivered to the customer and therefore also including re-used components.

Delphi Method

Extended expert estimate, where the subject matter is being assessed with finest granularity on the basis of the estimators' experience. It is characterized by a formalized process that involves multiple experts and a moderator.

Dynamic Baseline

Target value of a →benchmark, which has been derived by the values to be compared, for example, by calculating the average or median of these values.

Economy

In software development the minimization of duration and costs for systems or processes.

Effectiveness

Relationship of the objective reached to the objective defined.

Efficiency

Considers the profitability of a production process in terms of a cost-benefit ratio. In software development processes, it is defined as the ratio of output to input.

Elementary Process

Another name for a →base functional component as defined by →ISO/IEC 14143.

EN ISO 9000

Family of standards defining principles of quality management.

Expert Estimation

Effort estimation of multiple persons on the basis of their experiences and by comparing with already performed similar development tasks.

Explicit Requirement

Requirement which has been agreed on explicitly with the customer or product owner and has been documented comprehensibly.

External Benchmark

→Benchmark for the comparison of own metrics with those of other organisations.

Full Function Points Method

Also: FFP method. Original name of the →COSMIC method.

Function Point Analysis

Also: FPA. Method for measuring the size of software by counting →elementary processes and data structures related to →use cases. Standardized by the norm →ISO/IEC 20926.

Functional Requirement

Also: Functional User Requirement, FUR. Specifies a desired behavior of the running system related to its →use cases.

Functional Size Measurement

Also: FSM. Method for measuring the size of software on basis of →functional requirements. Standardized by the norm →ISO/IEC 14143

Functional User

Extended definition of an →actor. A functional user can be a human user, an external system or any input or output device.

Further Development Productivity

→Productivity of the process for the further development of an existing system.

IFPUG

Abbreviation for the International Function Point Users Group, a non-profit world-wide organization for the standardization and promotion of the →function point analysis.

Implicit Requirement

Common expectation regarding a non-functional characteristics where the requirement has not been →explicitly agreed on and documented.

Incremental Development

Type of software development where parts of a system are developed at different times and the system is extended by already completed parts.

Individual Software

Software, which has been created to fulfil the specific requirements of a particular customer.

Industrial Software Development

Software development using methods of the industrial production, in particular standardization, and reuse, automation and performance as well as quality measurements.

Innovation

The economic implementation of a product or service based on a new idea or invention.

Innovation Competition

Impact of the market dynamics caused by the internet where companies stand out from the crowd of competitors primariliy due to innovations.

Interactional Complexity

Complexity of →use case related interactions of →actors with a considered system.

Internal Benchmark

→Benchmark for the comparison of metrics coming from entities of the own organisation.

Interval Scale

Metric scale where different levels are defined by intervals of measurements.

ISO/IEC 14143

Standard for →functional size measurement

ISO/IEC 19761

Standard for →COSMIC method

ISO/IEC 20926

Standard for →function point analysis

ISO/IEC 25010

Standard for software quality. Defines software quality characteristics and their partition into sub-characteristics. Formerly: ISO/IEC 9126.

Iterative Development

Step-by-step refinement of implementing requirements, often starting with sophisticated and risky requirements and approximating the system closer to the objective with each iteration.

Key Performance Area

Also: KPA. Area with an impact on a specific process or product characteristics. The targeted improvement of a →key performance indicator requires knowledge of the KPAs which have a strong impact on KPIs.

Key Performance Indicator

Also: KPI. In the context of IT management the resulting value of a method measuring the progress of a process or product characteristics.

Knowledge Work

Type of work which requires knowledge to be successful. This can be by knowledge already acquired by the worker (implicit knowledge), new knowledge which the worker learns specially for his task, or explicit knowledge which the worker researchs or which will be provided by a knowledge management process.

Kondratiev Cycles

Cycles of the economic development which are, according to a model of the economist Nikolai Kondratiev, triggered by →innovations.

Line-of-Code Metric

→Size metric counting lines of the source code.

Maintainability

Criteria for the success and effort of changes. There are metrics which can be used as an indicator for the maintainability of a system. Poor maintainability has an impact on →further development productivity.

Management Model

Schema for implementing a →management system.

Management System

Framework for management tasks within a particular context including methods for monitoring and controlling the achievment of objectives.

Metric

In this context: Software metric. Function for mapping a specific process or product characteristics to a numerical value.

Milestone

A specific date of special significance within a development process. Usually the completion or delivery date of a specific artefact.

Milestone Trend Analysis

Also: MTA. Specific →milestones of the project plan are tracked over a longer period. From the trend of their postponements the probability of postponements of other milestones will be derived.

New Development Productivity

→Productivity of the process for the development of a new system.

Non-functional Requirement

Also: Non-functional User Requirement, NFUR. Specifies the expected characteristics of a product according to →ISO/IEC 25010.

Object Management Group

Also: OMG. Consortium for the development and maintenance of standards for vendor-independent, object-oriented modeling [OMG 2015].

Objectivity

A →metric is objective if the measured values are independent of the measuring person.

Persistence

Ability of a system to keep data (objects, states) or logical connections over a long period, in particular beyond a program abortion.

Process Metric

A →metric for measuring a characteristic of a process. →Productivity is a process metric for measuring the →efficiency.

Productivity

A →process metric. In software development →efficiency is usually considered as productivity.

Quality

Degree of fulfilment of →explicit and →implicit requirements.

Quality Assurance, analytical

Generic term for all activities related to searching, fixing and tracking →defects.

Quality Assurance, constructive

Generic term for all activities related to preventing →defects, for example by pre-defind processes, methods, guidelines, tools, and so on.

Quality Assurance, organizational

Generic term for the support of quality by expert roles and panels, for example, business or technical committees, security experts, subject matter experts, controlling boards or a steering committee.

Quality Characteristic

Property of →quality. The standard →ISO/IEC 25010 describes software quality characteristics.

Quality Gate

A →milestone in the course of a project where continuation or completion depends on the compliance with defined quality criteria.

Redesign

Structural improvement of the →Application Architecture without changes of the functionality.

Refactoring

Structural improvement of the code without changes of the functionality.

Release

New version of an application.

Reliability

A →metric is reliable if repeated measurements of the same object always come to the same result.

Return on Investment

Also: RoI. Model for the determination of the return of an entrepreneurial activity on the basis of the relationship of profit and invested capital.

Root Cause Analysis

Method for identifying the cause at the beginning of a cause-effect chain of a →defect.

Size Metric

A →metric for measuring the size of an IT system. Depending on the measuring method, the result can refer to the functional size, the program length, and so on.

Standard Software

Contrary to →individual software, standard software fulfills uniform requirements of numerous customers.

System Architecture

Definition of a system's internal construction by components such as applications, interfaces, database management systems, application servers, and so on.

Technical Debt

Negligence in the new development of a system. Impacts are insufficient →maintainability and poor →further development productivity.

Test Automation

Automated execution of test cases. Possible with unit tests, end-to-end tests and load tests.

Test Coverage

A →metric for measuring the percentage of →elementary processes, branches of the program flowchart, code lines, and so on which have been checked for →defects.

Time-based Competition

Also: TBC. The focus of providers of products and services in the internet on the time until the market entry (time to market) as a strategic competitive advantage.

Time Gap

The dilemma caused by the market dynamics in the internet (→time-based competition) on one side and the increasing complexity of new products and services that give competitive advantages on the other side.

Use Case

Use cases describe all scenarios of how →actors can accomplish specific goals by using a considered system. Each use case is defined by →elementary processes defining interactions between actors and the system abstracted from specific technical solutions [Cockburn 2002].

Validity

A →metric is valid, if the measured values represent the characteristics to be measured.

Virtualization

Simulation of a physical object or a resource using IT.

Bibliography

Cockburn 2002 Alistair Cockburn (2002): „Use cases, ten years later". URL http://a.cockburn.us/2098 (11.02.2015).

COSMIC FSM 2014 COSMIC FSM (2014): „The COSMIC Functional Size Measurement Method Version 4.0; Measurement Manual; The COSMIC Implementation Guide for ISO/IEC 19761:2011".URL http://www.cosmicon.com/portal/public/MM4.pdf (11.02.12015).

Fettke/Loos/Viehweger 2003 Peter Fettke/Peter Loos/Björn Viehweger (2003): „Komponentenmarktplätze – Bestandsaufnahme und Typologie". Johannes Gutenberg-Universität Mainz & Technische Universität Chemnitz, Feb 2003. URL http://www.fachkomponenten.de/docs/wkba5/b1.pdf (29.04.2015).

GitHub 2015 GitHub Inc. (2015): Product Website „Cobertura - A code coverage utility for Java". URL https://github.com/cobertura/cobertura (12.02.2015).

ISO/IEC 14143 2007 ISO/IEC 14143-1:2007 (2007): „Information technology -- Software measurement -- Functional size measurement -- Part 1: Definition of concepts". ISO (International Organization for Standardization).

ISO/IEC 20926 2009 ISO/IEC 20926:2009 (2009): „Software and systems engineering -- Software measurement -- IFPUG functional size measurement method 2009". ISO (International Organization for Standardization).

ISO/IEC 25010 2011 ISO/IEC 25010:2011 (2011): „Systems and software engineering -- Systems and software Quality Requirements and Evaluation (SQuaRE) -- System and software quality models". ISO (International Organization for Standardization).

Kamiske/Brauer 2007 Gerd F. Kamiske/ Jörg-Peter Brauer (2007): „Qualitätsmanagement von A - Z: Erläuterungen moderner Begriffe des Qualitätsmanagements". Carl Hanser Verlag.

Luckhaus 2014 Stefan Luckhaus (2014): „Produktivität in der Softwareentwicklung: Band 1 - Produktivitäts- und Leistungsmessung - Messbarkeit und Messmethoden". PASS IT-Consulting Dipl.-Inf. G. Rienecker GmbH & Co. KG.

Mountainminds 2015 Mountainminds (2015). Product Website „JaCoCo - Java Code Coverage for Eclipse". URL http://www.eclemma.org/jacoco (12.02.2015).

PASS 2013 PASS (2013): „Description of the PASS Data Interaction Point Method (DIP Method)". PASS Consulting Group (unpublished).

Selenium 2014 Selenium User Group (2014): Website „SeleniumHQ Browser Automation". URL http://docs.seleniumhq.org/ (30. 08 2014).

SonarSource 2014 SonarSource (2014): Product Website „SonarQube - Put your technical debt under control". URL http://www.sonarqube.org (12.02.2015).

Sondalini 2005 Mike Sondalini (2005): „RCFA and 5-Whys Tips for Successful Use". Lifetime Reliability Solutions. URL http://www.lifetime-reliability. com/free-articles/reliability-improvement/RCFA_and_5Whys_Tips.pdf (12.02.2015).

Tyto 2014 Tyto Software (2014): Vendor Wesite „Sahi - The Tester's Web Automation Tool". URL http://sahipro.com/ (30.08.2014).

Wallmüller 1990 Ernest Wallmüller (1990): „Software-Qualitätssicherung in der Praxis". Hanser Fachbuch.

About the Author

Stefan Luckhaus is a computer scientist with more than 35 years of experience. He has been working in software development since 1981 and graduated in Frankfurt in 1988, with the academic degree of Dipl.-Ing. (FH). Subsequently, he was a freelancer for 10 years. Since 1998, Stefan Luckhaus has been an employee of PASS Consulting Group. Initially working as a developer, he later managed development projects leading him to the USA, Singapore, India and various European countries. Today, Stefan Luckhaus is responsible for the competence center  Project Governance, providing process engineering for the software development of the entire PASS group. Here, he conducts productivity and quality measurements for more than 20 IT shops internally as well as on behalf of customers. He is a member of the PASS group's R&D unit and has the status of a principal innovation consultant.

Stefan Luckhaus' fields of expertise are software metrics, quality management and process models / engineering for software development. In the German ICT industry association BITKOM (Bundesverband Informationswirtschaft, Telekommunikation und neue Medien e.V.) he chairs the work group Quality Management, collaborated in the publication of „Agile Software Engineering Made in Germany" and is a speaker for example at the Bitkom Software Summits.

Stefan Luckhaus is present on the social networks LinkedIn, Xing and Twitter. He authors the blog www.software-productivity.com and co-authors the blog www.travel-industry-blog.com.

Book Recommendations

Stefan Luckhaus

Book Series
Increasing Productivity of Software Development

Part 1
Productivity and Performance Measurement – Measurability and Methods

How can software development become predictable, productive and reliable?

IT has changed almost all areas of life thanks to fundamental innovations. Our future will be dominated by virtualization and by smart helpers, that is, devices equipped with intelligence. Software is the stuff innovations are made of. Software development is a key competency.

The critical success factors for software developing enterprises are productivity and quality. Only suitable measuring methods and regular measurements enable these enterprises to estimate the effort for planned projects reliably and can set the foundation for a continuous improvement of productivity and quality.

This book describes practical experiences with measurements in software development: Pros and cons of established as well as novel methods, their automation, the impact of complexity and the steps towards their implentation.

ISBN

Hardcover: 978-3-9819565-6-6
Paperback: 978-3-9819565-8-0
e-Book: 978-3-9819565-7-3

Contents

Stefan Luckhaus

Cost Estimation in Agile Software Development
Utilizing Functional Size Measurement Methods

Whenever software is developed based on contracts with binding conditions such as the delivery of a clearly defined functional scope at a fixed price and at an agreed delivery date, it is exposed to risks. Many of these risks can be mitigated by the principles of agile development. Being able to navigate projects within all agreed parameters requires cost estimation methods to be integrated into planning and controlling processes. In order to prevent these methods from eroding the advantages of agile development, they must be rapidly applicable - ideally automatable - and allow for selfcalibration after every sprint.

This book illustrates, how size metrics can be utilised profitably in software development processes oriented towards agile values. It points out differences and restrictions, shows how the accuracy of cost estimations can be increased with each sprint and examines the feasibility of automated measurements.

ISBN

Hardcover: 978-3-7345-4372-2
Paperback: 978-3-7345-4371-5
e-Book: 978-3-7345-4373-9

Contents